D1373570

SKIING
BASICS

2-62

SKIING BASICS

Judy Crawford
with
Len Coates

Methuen/Two Continents

Toronto   New York   London   Sydney   Wellington

478 582Ar7

ISBN CANADA 0-458-91430-4 hc
                0-458-91420-7 pb
ISBN U.S.A.   0-8467-0158-8

Library of Congress
Catalog Card Number 75-39094
Printed and bound in Canada

Photos: John Nelson
Illustrations: David Simpson
Diagrams: Estfin Enterprises

1 2 3 4 5 WO 79 78 77 76

CONTENTS

PREFACE

For six years, Judy Crawford was ranked among the top women skiers in the world as a member of the Canadian National Ski Team. It was a blow to the team when she left to continue her education and to pursue a career in professional ski racing, but new challenges are important to Judy and she accepts them readily.

Her decision to accept the challenge of professional skiing is consistent with Judy's past record. At 16, she battled her way onto a team that included Olympic and World Cup gold medalist Nancy Greene. Judy was the youngest skier to be named to the Canadian team and the first from the flatlands of Ontario, which, topographically, is hardly suited to produce world class skiers.

Skiing Basics was also something of a challenge: to produce a no-nonsense approach to skiing, one that can benefit the beginner who desires the type of basic instruction from which he or she can go on to ski at any level.

As an instructor, a member of the Canadian Ski Instructors' Alliance, Judy is strong on basics, which is reflected in this book.

Len Coates
Ski Editor
Toronto Star

ACKNOWLEDGEMENTS

The authors would like to express their appreciation to Georgian Peaks Ski Club, Slalom Gate Ski Shop, Crystal Ski Shop and to David S. Reid Ltd., for providing Miss Crawford's ski wardrobe.

Chapter 1
INTRODUCTION

Skiing, to me, is competition. This holds true whether I'm racing against the best skiers in the world in Olympic or professional racing or just gliding down the hill on a Sunday afternoon with some friends. I believe most skiers feel this way.

On the World Cup trail, the object is to beat the other skiers, a tall order when you're skiing against Annemarie Proell or Gustavo Thoeni. And, of course, there's always that clock, inexorably ticking away the seconds.

The competitiveness of recreational skiing comes from striving to be the best skier on the hill. It can also come just from the desire to improve your own skiing, a competition with yourself to make every run and every turn better than the last. There is no such thing as a perfect run in skiing. There is no turn that couldn't have been a little bit better. And there's always a tougher mountain to challenge you when you've conquered the last one.

From the time I joined the Canadian National Ski Team at 16, there hasn't been much time for pleasure skiing. The opportunities I have had, though, have been a joy. I remember two occasions particularly, that recalled for me the great pleasure one can have from recreational skiing.

Following the 1974 World Series of Skiing in Vail, Colorado, we (the Canadian team) had a few days to free ski before heading home. Some friends had traveled down from Canada for the races and a ski holiday.

For two days, we chased one another over the mountains, leaping from cornices and, in general, just doing some crazy, wild skiing. The experience brought home to me how much I had missed skiing with friends, meeting people on the hill or chatting with them going up lifts. I'd forgotten what a delightful social experience skiing can be.

I recall vividly another time that demonstrated to me the pure delight and the sense of complete unrestricted freedom that skiing can bring. It happened at the end of my final season of World Cup skiing, when all the pressures of six years of training and competing were gone. Eight of us from the Canadian team took a helicopter into the Bugaboo range of the Canadian Rockies for a day of skiing on the glaciers.

We had the whole mountain to ourselves and the guide, after inspecting the glacier, let us go. He said, "There's no danger. The hill's yours."

Jim Hunter, of the Canadian men's team, an excellent athlete and superb downhill racer, led the way and I followed, turning Jungle Jim's zig-zag pattern into a chain of figure eights. We skied non-stop for five minutes in the deep powder of the glacier, then happily collapsed, weary but totally satisfied.

Skiing such as that, with people you like, is an experience you never forget.

I suppose I never would have been a recreational skier. I've never gone into anything without trying it competitively. Yet, I fully understand the attraction of free skiing.

The speed and movement provide a great feeling. Skiing gets you outside in the winter, a time of year that is far too good to waste hibernating in front of a TV set. If you ski, winter becomes a great time of year.

I've never found anything boring about skiing, even when I've been skiing on a hill all by myself. There's always a technical point to work on. The terrain is constantly changing. Moguls, or bumps, come and go. Weather and other skiers can make dramatic changes to a run within half-an-hour. For this reason, to me skiing is much more fun than swimming, for example, where the water in a pool never changes.

People who don't ski because they fear falls are missing a great deal. Properly equipped and properly clothed, even falls can be fun. You just dig yourself out of the snow, brush yourself off and go again.

The consequences of a fall or a mistake in recreational skiing are rarely serious. There is always the risk of injury, of course, but this can be minimized with proper equipment, conditioning and training. Usually, though, the price you pay for an error in recreational skiing is just a moment of awkwardness.

The penalty in ski racing is much more severe. The slightest mistake can make the difference between making the ski team or being an also-ran.

A tiny slip can cost time on a turn. The clock does not slow down while you recover.

In ski racing, the clock is the enemy. To become a successful ski racer, one must be totally aware of the penalties exacted by the clock for even the slightest mistake. In World Cup and all present forms of amateur racing, you are always racing against the clock. It's you against the sweep-second hand.

When I raced in the Olympics and on the World Cup tour, trying to beat a particular person was secondary to beating the clock. Naturally, some person sets the standard. But if Annemarie Proell or Monika Kaserer posted the fastest time in a slalom, it wasn't Annemarie or Monika I had to beat; it was the time they had posted. A time posted on a chalkboard may appear to be an impersonal thing, but it takes on the quality of a dreaded adversary.

Beating the clock, though, is only a part of it. You have to beat yourself, too, for ski racing is a constant struggle to improve your own performance.

This is particularly evident in Downhill time trials, held the day before a World Cup or Olympic Downhill race. Unlike slalom and giant slalom events, where you are not allowed to ski the course before the event, you have an opportunity to test your speed on a Downhill run before the race. You may ski the run several times and, in many cases, it's the same course you skied the year before, so you always have a standard — your own best time — to shoot for.

I recall at the end of every run my first concern was my time. I'd turn and look up at the clock as soon as the run was completed to see if I'd been faster. Only then, when I had beaten my own best time, did it ever occur to me to check to see who, among the Austrians, the Swiss, the Americans and even my own teammates, I had beaten.

I believe there are different competitive fires burning within the team player in sports, such as hockey, football and baseball, and the athlete involved in sports that are inherently individualistic, such as ski racing, tennis, golf and most track and field events.

Reporters often asked me why I raced, assuming, I suppose, that my answer would be full of patriotism for flag and homeland. I had to disappoint them.

Ski racing is an individual sport, a very personal thing. When you race, you race for yourself. You're rarely racing for your country or your sponsors. I believe everyone in ski racing feels that way. I'm sure Annemarie Proell, for example, raced for herself, not for Austria, although her victories certainly enhanced Austria's reputation in the sports world.

For the most part, ski racing is a matter of thinking about Judy Crawford beating her own best time. It's wanting Judy Crawford to do well. It's personal pride much more than patriotism.

Now, this doesn't mean that ski racers are totally selfish or that they are not well aware what they do in the Olympics or World Cup racing is a matter of national concern. I have seen the toughest competitors break down and cry like babies when their national flags were raised and their national anthems were played as they stood on the winner's podium. Many times I've felt a tear in my eye and a lump in my throat when one of my teammates won, and I've seen the same reaction from them when I did well.

Patriotic fever always runs high when you're traveling with the team and you're easily recognizable as the Canadian National Ski Team. Sometimes, a hotel where we stayed would hang a Canadian flag in the lobby or outside the hotel to welcome us and to show that the Canadians were staying there. It was a pleasing experience when that happened.

There's also much more patriotic zeal when skiing in an event such as the Nation's Cup, when individual performances are secondary to the team's showing. Then, it's Canada against the other teams.

We always had a strong rivalry with the U.S. National Ski Team in these events, probably because our language and common backgrounds brought us closer to the Americans than to skiers from other nations.

In Nation's Cup races, the object was very much to score points for Canada. And we always gave our best to be listed above the U.S. in the final standings. It was quite a serious matter.

I turned to professional ski racing for a number of reasons. After six years of World Cup racing, there didn't appear to be any new experiences for me in amateur racing. It wasn't changing, nor should it.

But, as an individual, new experiences are important for me and I think pro racing offers that opportunity. Ski racing becomes a lifestyle and, as a professional, I can continue in a sport very dear to me.

Chapter 2
CONDITIONING

You've heard it many times or read it often in the sports pages: "He played himself into shape." Well, maybe he did. But, if so, he probably didn't play very well. He certainly couldn't go all out. And if he was playing a sport that requires all-out exertion at any time, he was risking a serious injury.

It amazes me to see the number of skiers who think they can ski themselves into shape. Usually, they are so tired after a couple of runs that they are prime candidates for a fall. During a tumble, loose, poorly-conditioned tendons and ligaments are easily torn or overstrained. It can make for a short, but painful, ski season.

Statistics show that it's beginners who are most often injured while skiing, basically because they are not in condition. Experienced skiers know skiing is demanding, so usually they get into shape before the season starts. They also know that fatigue can cut into the precious hours they have to spend on the slopes.

Conditioning need not be torture, but it's just as important for the recreational skier as it is for the World Cup or professional racer.

It goes without saying that the legs are the single most important part of the anatomy to a skier; therefore conditioning should be concentrated here.

Running and cycling are both excellent exercises and, if possible, both should be included in any training program you devise. Running a mile a day or cycling three or four miles a day will do a lot to keep the ski patrol's stretcher away.

In addition, there are some exercises that are especially suited to ski conditioning. And all of them can be done in your own livingroom.

BURPIES

Burpies will help to develop the power you need in your legs and develop your wind. They are also an excellent all-around conditioner for any sport.

Start with two sets of ten burpies a day. Gradually, over a period of two weeks, work up to four sets a day.

Between each set, it's wise to rest until your pulse rate has slowed to 120 beats a minute, something you can easily count with a watch that has a sweep second hand.

Burpies

1. Start in a normal standing position with plenty of room behind you.

2. Bending at the knees, drop down until your palms are flat on the floor.

3. Now, thrust your legs straight back. Do it as hard as you can to stretch the leg muscles.

4. Again, with a snap, pull your legs back and resume the crouch position.

5. From the crouch, spring straight up into the air, throwing your arms up as high as you can reach. When you land, you should be in the normal standing position, ready to repeat the exercise.

SIT-UPS

Sooner or later, everyone loses their balance while skiing and the best hope of recovery before a fall depends on strong stomach muscles.

Apart from some of the tortuous things football players and boxers do to toughen up stomach muscles, the sit-up is probably the very best pre-season exercise for strengthening stomach muscles. There are three versions of the sit-up that I use for ski conditioning.

I'd recommend no more than 10 of each type each day to start, then gradually work up to 20 of each daily within a couple of weeks.

Sit-ups

1. Start the first two versions of the sit-up in the same manner: hands clasped behind the head; knees bent at a 45-degree angle; feet flat on the floor. You might find it necessary to have someone hold your feet down for the first few workouts, or hook them under a sofa or easychair to keep them on the floor.
2. In the first version, raise up and bring your underarms to meet your knees.
3. In the second version, add a twist so that your right underarm touches your left knee, then alternate. This brings into play some different muscles.

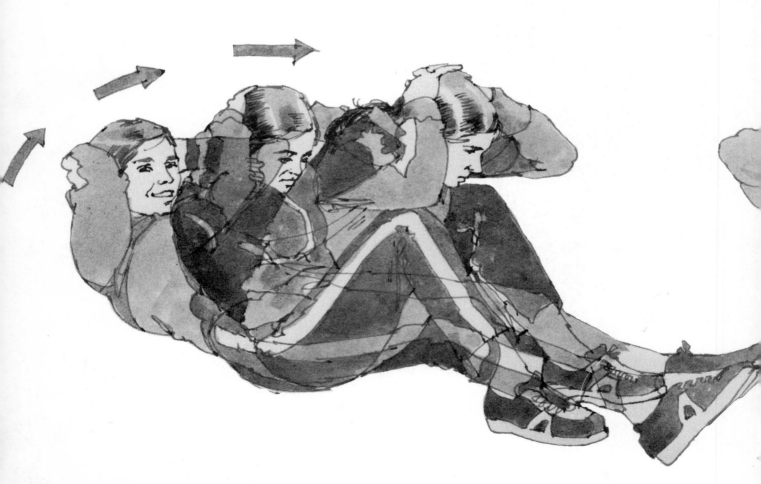

4. The third version is considerably more difficult and requires some strength and some balancing. Start with the body fully extended on the floor. Raise the upper body at the same time as you bring the knees up to meet the chest. Your own personal balancing point will become evident after a few tries. If you need even more variety, or more challenge, try keeping your feet raised off the floor as you go back to the extended position. This is tough, but it really works to get the **stomach** muscles in shape.

BENCH HOPS

The bench hop is an exercise especially suited for skiing, one that develops quickness, agility, balance, stamina and strength—in other words, everything you are going to need for safe, enjoyable skiing. In fact, the bench hop is probably the best ski exercise I know and should be kept up right through the ski season.

Racers use a bench — thus the name of the exercise — but perhaps a pillow will be high enough to start with. As your legs get stronger, pile on another pillow or find a small cardboard box. Finally, if you get really good, move up to a footstool or a bench. Go back and forth 20 times. Then try another 20.

Probably the greatest benefit of the bench hop, and all these exercises for that matter, is that they develop stamina. With endurance, you can ski down the hill with fewer rest stops, which makes it considerably easier to develop a rhythm in your skiing, which in turn increases your enjoyment and improves your skiing skills.

Bench hops

1. Start in a skiing stance with knees bent and feet six to eight inches apart. Push up, as much as possible, with both legs.

2. Throughout the exercise, keep the upper body quiet; that is, maintain the ski position throughout and let the legs do the work of getting you over the bench. Also, keep your hands in front of you.

3. Get a rhythm going in your hops, and try to land lightly on the balls of your feet.

Chapter 3
SKI EQUIPMENT

It almost goes without saying that the ski racer must have good equipment to be successful. But choosing the right equipment is even more important for the beginner. At least the racer has developed some skills and can make even the worst equipment work. The beginner doesn't have those skills and, what's more, incorrect, ill-fitting equipment will help to ensure they are never developed.

Ski equipment can be broken down into five categories: 1. Skis; 2. Boots; 3. Bindings; 4. Poles and accessories; 5. Clothing.

Ski clothing

Some people don't consider clothing as part of their equipment, arguing that what you wear has no effect on the way you ski. But they are wrong. Clothing that doesn't keep you warm or restricts your movements can have a serious detrimental effect on how you perform on the hill. An otherwise perfect day of skiing will be ruined if you are cold.

Therefore, let's establish a couple of basic rules for any skiwear:
1. It must be warm.
2. It must allow freedom of movement.

With the technology that has gone into the development of modern skiwear, there's no need to sacrifice warmth and freedom for style. Good-looking, smartly styled clothing is on the market and it's designed to move with you instead of against you and to keep you warm even in sub-zero temperatures.

A good rule of thumb is to prepare for the coldest possible weather when you go skiing. Often, conditions change dramatically during the day or even in the time it takes you to get from your home to the hill.

Many times I've talked to shivering skiers and heard them lament the fact that they had left their heavy ski jacket at home because the weather seemed so warm. How easy it would have been for them to put the jacket in the car, just in case. If the weather suddenly turns cold and your best jacket is at home in the closet, you'll be cold and your day will be ruined.

The first and most important item you'll need is a good, warm ski jacket that allows plenty of movement. Down-filled jackets are both light and warm. In the store, trying it on, flail around in it to make sure it isn't inhibiting. Stretch to your full length and even bend over to touch your toes to make sure it doesn't creep up around your shoulders.

Many beginners can't afford to buy ski pants and, true, they are costly and not an absolute necessity. But good ski pants keep you dry and allow you to stretch, two advantages they have over jeans or ordinary pants.

The latest designs also include an over-boot feature, which brings the pant leg over the top of the ski boot and keeps it there with a loop that fits over the first buckle of the boot, preventing snow from getting into the top of the boot.

Again, it's a good idea to try on pants in the store, then go through a series of gyrations that will confirm the pants stretchability. Don't be afraid to give them a real workout in the store, even if the salesperson stares at you or other customers gawk a bit. No workout you can give them in a store will compare with what they are going to suffer on the hills, and the stares are nothing to what you would get coming down the hill with split pants.

Lightweight thermal socks are recommended and, with modern boots that fit properly, the lighter the better. The problem these days with new boots is not that your feet get cold, even in below-zero skiing, but that they get too warm. Perspiration then becomes a problem. Naturally, any athletic sock should be able to absorb perspiration.

The range of gloves and mitts on the market is staggering. Gloves are more stylish, but mitts are warmer on the hands. I prefer gloves when skiing in competition, but in cold weather my hands ache, so I use mitts. I've noticed that many top international ski stars feel the same way, willing to sacrifice a bit of style for comfort. Leather mitts are almost a must, especially if there is any chance you will be riding a rope tow. Ropes will make short work of wool or fabric mitts. It's a good idea to get mitts a bit larger than you really need so that an extra pair of lightweight gloves can be slipped into them.

Underwear? I've heard hardy or foolish souls claim that long underwear is for sissies. I can't imagine skiing without my long, thermal underwear. I guess I'd rather be a comfortable sissy than a brave iceberg.

Next, a hat. They come in all shapes and sizes and personal taste will probably dictate what you'll buy. One that pulls down over the ears, though, is a must.

The glare of the sun off snow can be a serious hazard, so good sunglasses or tinted goggles are a must. Style, again, will probably play a big part in your choice, but I prefer polaroid lenses for almost all conditions, although I will occasionally switch to a yellow lens to give the bumps definition, if light conditions deteriorate to the point where there is no shadow on the snow.

A shell or light windproof jacket is a good idea for those days when a down-filled jacket is too warm. A shell keeps out the wind but doesn't let you become overly warm. Besides, it's something you can use all year round for tennis or sailing or just for casual outings in the spring and fall.

More and more warmup suits are appearing in ski shops and on the hills. They are a great boon on those very cold days, but invariably they become too hot in the spring or if you are lucky enough to be skiing on a warm winter afternoon.

It is nonsense to try to dictate what people must wear on the ski hill. They will wear what suits their budget and personal taste no matter what the so-called experts say. If nothing else, though, make this a rule of thumb: whenever you go skiing, prepare for the coldest

weather imaginable. It may well be sunny and warm when you start out from the city, but conditions later in the day and a few miles away can change drastically.

If you start out just wearing a shell or a sweater, leaving your ski jacket at home in the closet, you'll be cold and your day will be ruined if the weather changes. Take your warm clothes with you. It will pay off.

Skis

Beginners often ask me what kind of skis they should buy. The best advice I can give them is not to buy any at all.

In the first place, rushing out to buy skis, presuming you will like skiing, is foolish. You may not like it at all. Then you are stuck with a second-hand pair of skis worth about half what you paid for them, if, indeed, you can sell them at all.

Economically, then, it makes much more sense at the beginning to rent skis. It will also give you some experience with different lengths and other characteristics of skis that best suit your height, weight and skiing ability.

Because they are definitely easier to control, beginners should rent shorter skis to learn on, something in the area of 150 to 170 centimetres to start. Use short skis until you have mastered a few of the basics of skiing, then you can try slightly longer skis each time out as part of a learning process to discover the length that is best for you.

Length is one of the major considerations when it does come time to buy skis. But the stiffness of the ski is also important. Your first pair of skis will not be as long or as stiff as the skis you will ultimately end up with.

Length of your skis is a prime consideration, and there is enough variety on the market these days to suit every need. Usually beginners will start with shorter skis, and they are well advised to choose a pair that are not too stiff. Mid-priced fiberglass skis are probably the best bet. They will give you a couple of years of good service, by which time you will be ready to move into longer and stiffer skis. After two years, your old skis still have some trade-in or re-sale value.

Consider your first pair of skis as an intermediate step in your skiing development. You will grow out of them as your skills improve. Therefore, the first pair need not be top-of-the-line, which are not designed for beginners anyway. It makes no more sense for a beginner to buy the very best skis than it does for a novice racing driver to buy a Grand Prix racing car. The skis and the car will not be used anywhere near their maximum and the driver or skier could gain more knowledge from something much less sophisticated and costly. A mid-priced fiberglass ski is probably the best bet, because it will easily give you at least two years of service and will still have some re-sale value when it comes time to move up.

Because of the tremendous variety of skis on the market, any buyer must rely on a salesman for advice. Be absolutely candid about your ability. Many buyers defeat the purpose of soliciting advice by exaggerating their level, either upgrading it or downgrading it.

I've always found that ski shops located near ski areas, which are usually run by professionals, are good sources of information and guidance.

Boots

To my mind, choosing boots is much more important than your choice of skis. Nothing detracts more from your skiing enjoyment than a pair of uncomfortable, ill-fitting boots that don't provide the proper support.

Fit is the most important consideration when choosing boots, whether you are renting them for one day or buying them. They must be comfortable. If they cramp your foot, pinch or slop around when you are trying them on in the store, they will unquestionably cause you a great deal more agony on the hill.

Take along your own socks, the ones you will ski in, when you are trying on boots. At the store or ski shop, try them on and walk around in the boots for as long as necessary — at least a half-hour if you're buying—before you even consider them. Don't believe any salesman who tells you they will loosen up, or that they can be stretched, or that once you are on the hill they won't hurt.

Boots that are too loose are almost as bad as boots that are too tight. They will rub, causing blisters, and won't provide the proper support. A good test is to buckle up the boots, then lean forward in them with the boot flat on floor. You should be able to transfer all your weight to the balls of your feet and lean forward until you lose your balance without your heels raising up in the boot. The sole of your heels should stay firmly in contact with the bottom of the boot.

When you've determined the price and quality range to suit your requirements, try on as many brands as necessary to get a perfect fit. If Store A hasn't got the right brand to fit you, try Store B's brands. And don't buy a brand just because a friend recommends them or because a champion racer uses them. Buy it because it fits you.

Ski boots are designed to fit a skier's ability, just as skis are, so don't buy a boot that is out of your class. Even if you like the style or can afford the latest "trick" boot, you'll actually ski better and probably be more comfortable in a boot designed for your level of skiing. Racing boots are just as inappropriate for the beginner as beginner's boots are for the racer.

Almost all of today's boots are a plastic-compound outer shell with some form of inner liner for support, warmth and cushioning.

Most liners on contemporary boots contain a flowing material which softens when it contacts the warmth of your foot. Thus, the liner forms itself to fit your foot.

Other boots contain liners which are injected into the boot at the time of purchase while your foot is in the boot. The liner goes in as a foam, then is allowed to harden and, so the theory goes, exactly fits the contours of your foot. These are called "foam" boots. They are not necessary if you can find a boot that fits to begin with. I would only recommend them as a last resort if you find you are impossible to fit with a conventional boot.

Fit is the most important consideration when choosing boots. They must be comfortable. Buy boots that are designed for your level of skiing.

Bindings

While a binding is the most misunderstood and misused piece of equipment you will buy, it is also the most important. Consider that a good binding, properly adjusted, can save you from a broken leg or worse, while a poor binding or one incorrectly adjusted will contribute to an injury.

Bindings are supposed to keep you in your skis most of the time. In the event of a fall, though, the most important function of a binding comes into play—to release you from the ski in time to prevent the ski from acting as a lever on your leg and causing painful injuries.

How well a binding works depends not only on its design but also on the way it's adjusted. The best engineered binding in the world is worse than useless — it's diabolical — if it's poorly adjusted.

There are some poorly engineered bindings on the market. So to reduce the risk of getting one, restrict your selection to top name brands. It's great to patronise struggling young companies, but not at the risk of your leg. Even when choosing from name brands, select a model that has been around long enough to have a proven record of performance. Again, it may be daring to act as a guinea pig, but not at the expense of a broken leg.

In picking a binding, it is wise to consult a competent ski shop pro. The pro can help you select from a range of bindings that best suits your size, strength and the type of skiing you plan to do, all important factors in the ultimate choice.

Perhaps more important, the ski shop can explain how the binding works and how it is adjusted. As well as insisting on a name brand with a good record, insist on a style that is easily adjusted. Then, make absolutely certain that you know how to set the binding and test it.

A binding is the most important piece of ski equipment you will buy because it can save you from serious injury. The variety is almost endless, but it is wise to stick with bindings that have a proven record of performance. Knowing your bindings — how they work and how they are adjusted — is as important as picking a good set. A competent ski shop pro is your best friend in helping you make a selection that suits your size, weight and level of skiing.

Every good binding is designed to release you from the ski when it is subjected to lateral (sideways or twisting) forces at both the heel and the toe and when vertical (upward) force is exerted at the heel.

A good ski shop can determine the best settings for you in your bindings. They can show you how to check them yourself or they can check them at the shop.

They should be adjusted every day before you start to ski. Settings can change as you handle your skis or pack them and unpack them.

When you buy the bindings, insist on instructions on their care and maintenance and, then, keep them in good working order.

Most ski areas—in fact, every area I've ever skied at—demand safety straps attached to your binding and your boot to prevent runaway skis.

Poles

There are four criteria for buying poles:
1. They should be light,
2. They should be sturdy,
3. They should have adjustable wrist straps,
4. They should be the right height.

To determine the height, turn the pole upside down and clasp the end so that the point just shows. Keep your arms in close to your body, then bend your elbow to make a 90-degree angle. In this position, the end of the pole should just touch the floor.

Poles should be light, sturdy, have adjustable wrist straps and should be the right height. Here's the proper way to determine the height best for you: clasp the pointed end as shown. The handle of the pole should be on the floor when your elbow is bent at a 90-degree angle.

Chapter 4
SKI LESSONS

On the following pages, I will attempt to present to you a clear, easily understood step-by-step method of learning to ski. It is not a ski-quick or instant-parallel approach. Rather, it's the tried and tested method authorized by every major ski instruction body in the world, including the Canadian Ski Instructors Alliance, of which I am a member.

There are easier ways to learn to ski, frankly. Other methods and other books of instruction will promise to have you skiing parallel in a day, and they might well fulfill the promise. I won't teach that way because I happen to believe there is only one correct way to ski and there are no shortcuts to attain it.

There are basics to learn. To progress as far as you are able in skiing, it is necessary to learn the rudiments; to learn why a particular action on your part creates a predictable reaction by your skis.

I liken the quick-ski methods with learning to drive a car that has an automatic transmission or taking one of those learn-to-play-in-a-day piano courses. There's nothing wrong with them, mind you, as long as your requirements and demands are limited. But there are important ingredients missing. With them, you can develop only so far because you've skipped the basics upon which the ultimate expression of the art is predicated.

To my thinking, the ultimate expression of the art of skiing is demonstrated by ski racers, and every racer learned to ski by the time-honored method on the following pages.

Ready to go? Okay. Just check first, though, to make sure you haven't forgotten anything. From the top: Hat? Goggles? Warm jacket? Shell? Ski pants? Gloves or mitts? Thermal socks? Long underwear? Boots? Poles? Skis?

Everything checks. Let's go.

It will take some time to get accustomed to the feel of skis on your feet, so it is worthwhile to put them on and walk around the ski area before you attempt your first hill. As you walk, keep the weight on the balls of your feet. Don't take long steps to begin with. Keep your hands in front of you and look ahead, not at your feet. Above all, relax.

AT THE HILL

Don't start off by making the same mistake that many beginners do, which is being in too big a rush to get to the top of the mountain. Relax. Before anything else, you've got to get used to the feel of those skis and boots on your feet. It's going to take a little getting accustomed to — you've just added five or six feet onto the length of your normal street shoes.

Even before you buy a lift ticket, put on your skis and go for a walk around the ski area just to get the feel of things. As you walk, use your poles to push yourself along. Practice turning around until you can do it without getting your skis and poles all crossed up.

Walk on the balls of your feet. It's a good thing to practice right from the start because everything you are going to do in skiing is done on the balls of your feet.

Every once in awhile, use your poles to push yourself forward and glide to a stop. It will give you a feel of what it is like to be sliding on skis.

A wise skier perfects one step at a time. So, only when you begin to feel comfortable on your new "stretched feet" should you attempt to go on to the next step.

Before you get up on the hill and discover you and your skis are heading off in different directions, it makes a great deal of sense to wait until your skis begin to feel like a part of you. I can't count the number of times I've seen instructors trying to cope with someone who has just put on skis for the first time and headed directly for the top of the hill. Sometimes they can't even stand up on skis and here they are wasting their money and the instructor's time learning to stand up and walk on skis.

The walk around the area also serves another important purpose. It will help you to choose your first hill. While you are getting used to those awkward boards on your feet, keep your eyes open for a short gradual incline. The best choice for your first attempt to come down a hill should also be smooth and wide, with any trees well off to the side.

For this first hill, forget the ski lift. Climb it, using the side-step method. The wisdom of this move will soon be apparent. Sometime very soon, you will drop a glove or ski pole in the middle of the hill and have to climb back up to retrieve it. Besides, a short climb is a good warmup to stretch muscles, one that is even used by ski racers before practice or a race.

To get the feel of gliding on skis, push yourself along and slide to a stop. Use both hands equally. As you push, don't let your hands go too far behind you.

The step-up, or side-step climb, is handy to know even before you get up the hill. Make sure the lower ski is stable and, to begin, keep all your weight on the lower ski and pole. Lift the uphill ski and pole and step up. Then transfer your weight to the uphill ski, at the same time using the planted downhill pole to push on. When the step is completed, bring the downhill ski up to meet the uphill ski.

The other basic climbing method is the herringbone, so named because of the pattern you will leave in the snow. It's the short, quick method used for gradual inclines. It is not used on steep hills. You are stepping up the hill with the skis at the angle shown, as sharp as possible. You must push with the poles to help you step up and to keep you from sliding back down the hill.

SNOWPLOW POSITION

The basic beginner position is called the snowplow, for reasons that will become obvious. The tips of the skis should be together, almost touching. The tails or backs of the skis should be fanned out behind, spread far enough apart to allow your knees to bend comfortably.

Those bent knees are very important, probably the most important part of skiing. All skiing—everything you will ever learn—is based on bending or unbending the knees, an action called flexion. Flex your knees several times to be sure they bend easily and comfortably.

Also remember, you are on the balls of your feet and you are bending your knees by pushing forward, not just dropping your posterior closer to the ground.

This is the proper snowplow position: tips of the skis are almost together; tails are fanned out behind; knees are bent; you are on the balls of your feet; and your hands are out in front, about shoulder-width apart.

Your hands should be held comfortably in front of you, raised so you can see them as you slide down the hill. Hold them about shoulder-width apart.

Your poles will simply trail along behind you for the moment.

Understand that the snowplow is basically a method of controlling your speed on the hill. The principle is simply to get the skis to act like the blades of a snowplow, thus creating resistance against their natural inclination to slide directly to the bottom.

Imagine, for instance, if plow blades were lying flat on the hill. They would be free to slip all the way down the mountain. Angled, though, the blades dig into the snow, slowing the plow and eventually, if the angle is great enough, stopping it.

On skis, you create the desired angle by exerting pressure in with the knees and out at the heels. This causes a slight lift of the outside edges and the inside edges dig into the snow.

The angle of the skis comes from bending your knees. The more the knees bend, the greater the angle, and thus the more the skis dig into the snow. Here the knees are well bent, putting the skis at an angle that will slow you quickly or bring you to a stop.

Start the snowplow exercise in the normal running position, skis parallel, about four or five inches apart.

Before you try it on a hill, you can practice the snowplow action on a flat at the top of the hill. Do the snowplow exercise a couple of times, each time increasing the angle of the skis by exerting more pressure in at the knees and out at the heels.

Now, comes the big moment. You should be ready to try your first hill. Wait until the way is clear, then push off in the snowplow position.

As you start to slide, you will discover you can control your speed by the amount of pressure you exert to make those inside edges bite into the snow. To increase your speed, you simply ease the pressure. The skis flatten out and you begin to slide faster. Apply pressure and you slow. More pressure and you stop.

Push out at the heels and apply pressure through the knees by pushing forward and in toward the center. The skis should slide out at the tails into the snowplow position.

For this first hill, try to ski as slowly as you can, stopping a couple of times on the way down. Watch for other skiers, especially other beginners, ahead of you and keep your speed well under control in case someone suddenly stops or falls in front of you.

When you make it to the bottom, you are ready to try your first ski lift.

Try the hill at least a half-dozen times, each time stopping several times on the way down, but also slowly increasing your speed each time. Make sure you feel comfortable at one speed before you increase the rate of your descent. And, always, ski at a speed you feel you can easily control.

1 2

3 4

SNOWPLOW TURN

The snowplow turn is the basic turn in skiing and the basis for all the turns you will ever learn.

Start down the hill in the snowplow position. To begin to make the turn, you must gradually shift most of your weight onto one ski. At the same time, you must change the angle of the "weighted ski" so that the edge carves into the snow. This is accomplished by applying pressure with the knee, an action we call knee-drive.

Let's try a left turn step-by-step, which means you will be using the right ski — the opposite one to the direction of the turn — as the weighted ski.

Here we go. Step one is gradually to shift your weight onto your right ski and, at the same time, begin to apply pressure to edge the ski, driving forward and inward with the right knee.

Step two is done for you. When your weight is solidly over the right ski and the ski is edged, it cuts into the snow and it turns automatically.

Step three. As the turn is completed, transfer your weight back until it is more evenly distributed over both skis and ease the pressure from your knee.

You will now be skiing across the hill, which is called traversing, a term you will hear often. During the traverse, most of your weight will be on the downhill ski.

When you pass the fall line — another common term referring to an imaginery line a ball would follow if rolled from the top of the hill — you should begin to prepare to turn the other way by starting to shift your weight to the left ski.

At this stage, don't rush. It will take lots of practice before you can come down the hill easily and smoothly, turning, traversing, then turning the other way. Gradually, you can shorten the traverse and bring your turns in closer to the fall line.

Snowplow Turn:

1. Start in the normal snowplow position; look ahead and gradually begin to shift your weight over the left leg (to make a right turn).

2. As your weight is shifted to the left ski, push the knee in and forward to edge the ski.

3. Pressure at the knee will control the arc of the turn; make the turn big and round.

4. As the turn is completed, ease the pressure at the knee and you will return to a straight run.

A proper pole plant is made with the arm extended well out in front of you. Just touch the snow lightly and lift the pole back. You should be attempting to turn around the spot where the pole was planted, not turning around the pole itself. If the pole gets behind you, like this, it will throw you off balance.

POLE PLANT

In learning to ski, some things you just have to take on faith, accepting that the instructor knows what he or she is doing and has some grand design in mind. Such is the pole plant. Beginners usually find it difficult to understand why they should plant a pole before a turn. What does it do?

It does two things. One, it's a signal to yourself to initiate a turn. Secondly, and more important, it achieves a balance that is essential in turns you will learn later.

Planting the pole should begin when you have mastered the snowplow turn and feel comfortable with it. True, at this stage, the pole

plant doesn't appear to be doing anything for you at all. But it's wise to make it a habit now. The wisdom will become obvious later. Have faith.

As you prepare to make a turn, extend the arm holding the downhill pole and place the pole lightly in the snow. It's just a light touch on the snow, then the pole is lifted as you pass.

You should be trying to turn around the spot where the pole was planted, not trying to turn around the pole itself. You are not trying to pivot around the pole, using your arm as an axis. This is a sure way to throw yourself off balance.

Another mistake commonly made that will also cost you your balance is to let your hands get behind you before you lift the pole out of the snow.

Perhaps, at first, the pole plant seems awkward and unnecessary, but soon it becomes second nature and, you'll see, it improves your balance.

After completing a normal snowplow turn, slide the uphill ski down to meet the downhill ski so they are running parallel as you cross the hill.

CHRISTIE TURN

The Christie — sometimes also known as the Stem Christie — is the intermediate step between the snowplow turn and the parallel turn.

When you have completed a snowplow turn, instead of traversing the hill in the snowplow position, slide your uphill ski down to meet the downhill ski. Now, you will be traversing the hill in the normal running position; your skis running parallel and about shoulder-width apart for good balance. You should have your weight on the downhill ski.

Return to the snowplow position for the next turn by stepping up into position with the uphill ski. This should be fairly easy because all your weight is on the downhill ski. Now, to initiate the turn, begin to shift your weight to the uphill ski exactly as you have been doing for the snowplow turn. As you complete the turn, again slide your uphill ski down to meet the downhill ski.

Crossing the hill in this fashion is called a traverse. To prepare for the next turn, shift your weight to the downhill ski and step the uphill ski back into the snowplow position and complete the turn.

Initially, the Christie is made up of several distinct moves: step up; turn; step down; traverse; step up again. The next step is to simply make it smooth until, gradually, the return to the running position becomes part of the turn.

As you practice, it becomes easier and more natural to slide the uphill ski into position rather than step it to make the next turn. Again, as with the snowplow turn, when your Christies become smoother, shorten the traverse, bringing the turns in closer to the fall line.

1   2

MOVING TO PARALLEL

As traverses between Christie turns become shorter and shorter and the slide between the traverse and the turn becomes smoother, you will probably notice that you are getting very close to parallel skiing.

That's because there is no sudden, spectacular, one-step move to parallel skiing. Instead, it's a series of tiny changes in a Christie turn that will finally bring you to the parallel turn. It starts when you are traversing the hill in the normal running position, then shifting into a snowplow position to begin a Christie turn.

Gradually, now, you must shorten the step or slide until it disappears altogether. When the step is gone, you are turning parallel. To get to the parallel turn, a steering action from the feet must be brought into play. Your weight must be projected forward and slightly over the downhill ski to get the necessary knee-drive.

It won't happen, though, unless you are using the knees. It's pressure with the knees — knee-drive — that puts the skis on edge, getting them to carve and turn.

Knee-drive is the key. Try it during a traverse. Drive your knees toward the hill and you'll immediately feel the reaction on your skis. Throughout this period—admittedly a difficult one in learning to ski— you must consciously accentuate the knee-drive. Make it a strong forward push toward the direction of the turn. It helps to keep your weight well forward on the balls of your feet.

As your Christie moves closer to parallel, remember to keep your feet at least four-to-five inches apart. Later, when your balance is better, you can bring them closer if you wish.

3

4

5

6

1. *The key to the parallel turn is knee drive. Here you can see that by driving the knees forward and in the direction of the turn, you are putting the skis on edge so they are able to carve the turn.*

2. *Begin the turn from the traverse position.*

3. *Plant the pole and begin to shift the weight to the uphill ski.*

4. *Apply pressure with the knees to get the skis on edge. Keep your arms ahead and your weight on the uphill or outside ski.*

5. *With your weight on the uphill ski and with your knees driving to get edging, the skis do the turning.*

6. *Continue the knee-drive until the turn is fully completed and you are once again traversing the hill.*

STOPPING

As your skiing becomes more proficient, you will want to try longer and steeper hills. Now, stopping quickly and surely will become more important.

There are two basic methods of stopping on skis. One of them, you already know, is our old friend the snowplow. The snowplow stop works well in many instances. However, it is not the most efficient or quickest way to stop.

In fact, snowplow stops can be dangerous when you are traveling very fast because your legs in that position can't absorb the forces, and edges catch very easily. The snowplow is handy when there's not enough room to make a normal downhill stop, sometimes called a hockey stop. Anyone who skates is probably very familiar with the movement.

The downhill stop is a quick throwing of the skis sideways. You bring the tails of the skis around and, with strong knee-drive, get the skis up on their edges. Almost all of the weight is on the downhill ski

The downhill stop is a quick throwing of the skis sideways. The weight should be on the downhill ski and the knees should be well bent and pushing forward. Push the heels of the skis around. Keep your body pointing downhill so that you do not turn right around. Make sure the downhill pole is raised out of the way.

and the more knee-drive you use, the faster you will stop. It's important to keep your body facing downhill as you stop, or you are liable to spin completely around.

Here's another most important warning: no matter how drastic the situation, never attempt to stop by falling down. It's a most inefficient way to slow down, much inferior to using the edges of your skis. It is especially dangerous to sit down. You will then simply be riding on the backs of your skis and you'll probably slide right into the thing you were trying to avoid.

KEEPING THE BODY QUIET

As much as possible in skiing, move only from the waist down, always keeping the upper body angled toward the bottom of the hill.

Although we learned to keep the body pointed in line with the skis when we were skiing snowplow, the habit now must be broken. If you rotate the torso to follow the skis when you are skiing parallel, you will be thrown off balance.

In skiing, every movement of the upper body is transmitted to the skis; therefore it is important to keep the upper body quiet. Keep your arms in front, only moving to make a pole plant. Don't flail your arms or rotate your torso—either action takes the weight off the edges of your skis.

In fact, every time you move your upper body or arms while skiing, it has effect on the skis, usually adverse and often disastrous. Even though you are making the correct moves with your lower body, all the good you are doing can be washed out by movements of the arms and upper body.

Therefore, it is important to keep the upper body quiet. This means your arms should be restricted to the pole plant and even this should be performed with an economy of movement. Don't flail about. Keep your arms in front of you and keep them quiet. They have a job to do and every extra movement detracts from that job.

The same is true of the torso. If it is rotating, it takes weight off the edges of the skis and makes the backs of the skis slide rather than carve.

Did you ever stand at the bottom of a ski hill and wonder why some skiers look so much smoother than others. They make the whole thing look easy. Watch them closely the next time. They look good because they are not flapping around.

FIVE COMMON ERRORS

Sometimes the best way to learn is to remember the Do Nots. Here are the five most common faults I see on the hill:

1. Throwing the hip Many skiers confuse "throwing the hip" with knee-drive. In fact, it actually retards knee-drive and it forces you to move your entire body the other way to start your next turn.

The hips must not be allowed to get out of line. They should always be squarely over the skis. The next time you make a turn, try to catch yourself with your hip thrown out to the side. Then get working to get them back over the skis. It's an extra and wasteful movement.

2. Not fully completing a turn Sliding sideways is inefficient, sloppy and it slows you down, yet many skiers allow their skis to slide through the latter part of a turn, rather than carve the turn through to its completion.

They stop carving because their knee-drive quits before the turn is completed.

Check yourself by studying the track you leave in the snow. If it is a nicely carved track, clearly showing two distinct lines, then you have little to worry about. On the other hand, if it shows your skis were slipping out at the end of the turn, you know you've been lazy. Keep your knees driving until the turn is fully completed.

3. Up-Down syndrome This is the tendency for skiers to go from a full-body extension to a low crouch as they weight and unweight in turns. It's to be avoided at all costs, especially on ice because a full extension will take the weight almost completely off the skis. You quickly lose contact with the snow or ice and start to slip sideways.

The Down, or full crouch, is simply a lot of wasted effort and often puts the weight on the backs of the skis when it should be up front.

Your control in skiing should come from knee-drive, which can produce the effect of weighting and unweighting much more efficiently than the Up-Down. Using the knees, it is much easier to keep your weight firmly on your edges so you maintain much better control.

Under normal snow conditions, there should be only a little Up-Down to effect a rhythm in your skiing. In deep powder, an exaggerated Up-Down is almost a necessity for rhythm, but even then it need not be a full extension to a low crouch.

4. Ski loose Fear is probably the skier's worst enemy because it causes you to become tense at a time when tightening up only serves to compound your problems.

I've seen it happen many times. A skier comes up on a patch of ice or another skier cuts him off. The first reaction is to shrink away, to physically pull back from the thing you fear.

If you do this, here is what happens and it is important to understand. When you pull back, you sit back on your skis. The weight goes to the back of the skis and the tips float. With the tips floating, it is impossible to get knee-drive and the ultimate result is a loss of control.

Often skiers in stress situations revert to body movements and this doesn't help either. Don't fool yourself into thinking that breaking at the waist (leaning forward with the upper body) is putting weight back on the front of the skis.

The only way to get the weight to the front of the skis is with knee-drive. Keep your weight on the balls of your feet, even in the most ticklish situation, then you can be sure the tips aren't going to float.

Heaven knows, I have felt fear many times in World Cup downhill races. But I also know that shrinking back is the worst possible reaction.

Stand up. Ski aggressively, and almost always you will get through with no harm.

5. Banking Banking means leaning into the hill with the entire body. Skiers make the mistake of thinking this increases edging by increasing the angle of the skis.

But the desired angle must come from knee-drive. Banking only removes the weight from over the downhill ski, causing it to slip sideways. Carried to an extreme, banking causes the downhill ski to slip out from under you and you fall.

1

2

3

Some DON'TS:

1. Don't bend forward at the waist. It's impossible to get proper knee drive. Keep upper body erect. Bending forward is often a product of fear, but it increases the problem you feared in the first place.

2. Don't bank your body in a turn. It takes the weight off the outside ski.

3. Don't confuse throwing the hip with knee-drive. Keep the hips squarely over the skis or, as this shows, the thrown hip will shift the weight onto the uphill ski.

AVALEMENT

Literally translated, *avalement* means swallowing or gobbling up. In skiing, it is a technique that will allow you to gobble up moguls, or bumps. It is the technique of using your knees as shock absorbers.

The key to good control in mogul skiing is to keep your skis solidly in contact with the snow, all of which is determined in that critical moment as you approach and begin to rise over a mogul.

At this point, you should be in a high, almost fully upright position. As you start to hit the bump, allow your knees to come up while keeping the rest of your body on a fairly even plane. You should be absorbing the rise with your legs only.

As you come up to the top of the bump, it is natural that your weight has shifted to the rear of the skis. You don't want it there when you crest the mogul, so, at the top, push your weight forward toward the tips of the skis.

As the bump falls away, begin to extend your legs to keep in solid contact with the hill. This will also put you back in the upright position, ready for the next mogul.

Avalement is the technique of using your knees as shock absorbers to take a bump. As you approach the bump, the hands should be well ahead and the knees bent only slightly. As you reach the upper slope of the bump, the body should maintain an even plane while the legs take the bump. As the tips of your skis climb the bump, push your weight forward slightly.

At the crest, your knees should be well bent. At this point, push your weight all the way forward to keep the ski tips on the snow.

On the downside of the bump, you should still be pushing forward, but you should also be extending your legs as the bump drops away, which helps to reduce the shock on the downside.

ADJUSTING SKIING TO CONDITIONS

Much is made of adjusting your skiing to handle vastly different snow conditions. The best way, though, to handle any ski condition is to acquire a sound knowledge of skiing basics.

On ice, for instance, the basic errors will show up very quickly, especially weak edging or if you are forgetting to keep your weight on the downhill ski. Either fault wil result in your skis slipping out from under you and you will be heading for a fall.

Racers attack ice harder than normal snow conditions because they know when they are skiing aggressively they are concentrating on edging, thinking about where their weight is positioned and not worrying about falling down. Fear and timidity are your worst enemies on ice.

Deep powder requires you sit back farther on your skis to keep the tips out of the snow. It helps in powder to keep the feet close together to counteract a tendency for the snow to steer a loose ski. A more pronounced weighting and unweighting is necessary to develop a rhythm in deep powder.

On slush or wet spring snow, it is wise to remember that everything happens slower. Wax helps. Sit back, just a bit, so you are prepared when the skis suddenly slow in deep slush.

Chapter 5
SKI RACING

So far, we've talked about getting down the hill as smoothly and as precisely as possible. Now, we'll go on to getting down as quickly as possible. We'll also stick some poles in the snow for added interest and we'll ski around them.

In other words, ski racing.

The basics of skiing, the recreational variety, also apply to ski racing. The principles are the same. Thus a strong recreational skier, given the right temperment and competitive urges, should make a good ski racer.

In most countries, joining a ski club is the first step to becoming a racer. It is necessary to select a club that is affiliated with the national ski association, and it is best to choose one that has good coaching and takes its racing seriously.

By joining an affiliated ski club, you come under the umbrella of the world organizing body of skiing, the Federation Internationale de Ski (FIS).

The FIS is a federation of about 40 ski countries. It governs both Alpine racing and Nordic events (ski jumping and cross-country racing). Its various committees, made up of delegates from member national associations, make the rules, produce ski calendars for annual international competitions, rank ski racers and approve courses for international competition.

If you imagine the organizational chart of competitive skiing as a pyramid, then the FIS is right at the peak of the pyramid. The FIS secretariat is located in Stockholm, Sweden.

At the second level on the pyramid are the national governing bodies, such as the Canadian Ski Association (CSA) and the United States Ski Association (USSA).

The national associations are made up of divisions or zones and ski clubs in their areas come under the division umbrella.

Recreational skiing, liaison with fitness associations and tourist boards and close contact with the skiing industry are all functions of the FIS, national organizations and regional associations. But their main emphasis and most of their time and effort go into organizing ski racing from the World Cup and Olympic level right down to the club event for the youngest racers.

LEVELS OF RACING

The highest level of amateur racing in the world is World Cup Skiing, a series of events for both men and women that takes place in Europe and North America from December to March every year.

But there are many steps in the ski-racing ladder before a racer gets to that level.

Most racers start quite young (7 to 9), racing at the club level in house league races. Some think this is too young, but the key is that it should be low-pressure racing with the emphasis on fun and not on winning.

The better racers and club champions are usually selected for the club team and will race against the best from other clubs. Club racing and intra-club events are usually set up to cater to all age groups.

Division or zone teams are always on the lookout, though, for the best of the young skiers to stock the division squads.

From the division level, skiers move onto national teams and from there are assigned to either the World Cup squads or, in Europe, the Europa Cup teams, or in North America, the Can-Am series squads.

The Can-Am is a series of races between the Canadian and U.S. national "B" teams, usually made up of young racers who are trying to reach the World Cup level. It is the North American counterpart of the Europa Cup, in which European "B" teams compete against each other.

The goal, though, of every amateur skier is to make his or her country's World Cup squad. Some of the Alpine countries, such as Austria, Switzerland, Italy and France, carry as many as 30 to 40 skiers on the World Cup teams, while the North American teams usually have from 8 to 12 skiers. Some smaller countries may have only one or two racers on their teams.

It's from the World Cup squads that countries usually pick their skiers for Olympic competition, every four years. The Olympics are also counted as the world skiing championship in Olympic years, while a separate World Championship meet is held every four years by the FIS.

Unquestionably, the Olympics are the goal of every amateur skier and the world watches Olympic skiing with greater interest than any other ski competition.

Each country in the Olympics is allowed to enter four skiers in each discipline—downhill, slalom and giant slalom. The rewards are probably the most coveted in sports—a gold medal for first, silver for second and bronze for third place.

Only twice in Olympic history have skiers swept all three events. Austria's great star Toni Sailer was the first to win three gold in the 1956 Olympics at Cortina, Italy.

Jean-Claude Killy of France became the second triple gold medal winner at Grenoble, France, in 1968.

The World Championships are held on their own every four years, two years removed from the Olympics. Here, too, gold, silver and bronze medals are awarded to the first three skiers in each event.

The World Cup series, held every year, is usually made up of 27 events for men and 26 events for women. Points are awarded to the ten best skiers in each event on a scale of 25-20-15-11-8-6-4-3-2-1. At several selected events, combined standings, figured on a skier's placing in two events, can earn World Cup points.

A skier can only count results from 13 races in his or her points total. Recently, men have been allowed to count their 6 best results from the first 12 events in the series and their 7 best results from the

final 15 races. Women count 7 of the first 14 events and 6 of the final
12.

The man and woman with the best points total are awarded the World Cup, while medals are awarded to the top three skiers in each discipline, with their five best results in the respective category taken into consideration.

FIS Points

An international grading system of FIS points is used to seed skiers in FIS-sanctioned events, a very important matter because FIS points determine starting positions in racing events.

FIS Points are awarded on a descending scale, that is, the best skier in a World Cup event scores zero points. Everyone else in the race is assessed points according to the time difference between their clocking and the winning time.

Europa Cup, Can-Am, National championships and division races are also seeded according to FIS Points, but the scale is determined by the importance of the event. For instance, the winner of a Can-Am race or Europa race might be assessed 25 FIS points while all others receive more.

World Cup competition is open to men who have less than 30 FIS points and to women with less than 50. Apart from eligibility, the points come into play in the seeding system that determines starting positions in ski events.

For purposes of drawing starting positions, skiers are divided into groups of 15, with the top seeds — skiers with the lowest points and therefore likely to be the best — in the first seed or group.

These 15 skiers will always start first in any event. In a slalom or giant slalom and even in some downhills an early starting place is a tremendous advantage because it allows you on the course before it is chewed up by other skiers. Unfortunately for the young skier trying to make a place in international skiing, it's often a long, hard haul just to get into the top seed. Some, needless to say, never make it. It is very difficult to win when you are starting from the third or fourth seed, in fact, almost impossible in slalom and giant slalom.

THE RACING LIFE

Ski racing, whether it be World Cup, professional or for a division team, is almost a full time business. There hardly seems to be any summer. There's certainly never enough time for relaxation or studies, something that young skiers should carefully consider when they are contemplating a ski-racing career.

I've known some excellent skiers who've dropped from national teams or refused invitations to join teams because of the sacrifices in time and devotion to the sport. Their education or careers took precedence over ski racing.

Only very rarely can a racing career and other pursuits mix. Usually, those who try end up doing a poor job in both areas and, ultimately, they drop one.

The World Cup season starts in late November, but official training starts in the summer. Conditioning never ends and the wise ski racer is working all the time to stay in top condition and increase strength.

Let's look at a typical racing season.

From December to March, it's racing. At the Can-Am, World Cup and professional level, life develops a pattern: racing, packing, traveling to the next race, training and racing. Then it starts all over again.

Sure, it's a glamorous life, traveling around Europe and North America. But, it's also just plain hard work and, at times, boring routine. Only the love of skiing and competing makes up for the grind.

Apart from a couple of short summer racing camps, North American racers are off from April through to July. It's a time to go back to school to work toward graduation from high school or to cram a semester at college or university.

You are on your own to keep in condition during the summer and most ski racers develop a regular regimen of running, biking, conditioning games (squash, tennis, etc.). Regular visits to a gym for sit-ups, push-ups or weight training also pay off in increased strength and stamina for the long haul that starts in August.

National teams in Canada and the U.S. regularly schedule a couple of summer camps, basically to work on technique. The camps, usually five or six days each, are also designed to ensure you don't lose the touch or the feeling of skis.

They're held high in the Rockies on glaciers that remain all year round and, although you get the opportunity to ski gates a few times, I generally find summer camps boring, a series of brief runs on the short glaciers.

In the past few years, South America (Chile and Argentina) has become a popular place for major summer camps. These camps are from four to five weeks long, during which the team concentrates on downhill training.

There is an Australian men's racing circuit, where a racer can improve his FIS Points and get valuable experience in slalom and giant slalom races.

The South American camp is also the place where the coaches determine the rosters of the World Cup and Can-Am teams and where they chart the progress of young racers. A good training camp performance often means more than what a skier did the year before, especially in the case of the younger racers, some of whom develop very quickly indeed. One year can often make a tremendous difference in a skier's progress because young skiers tend to benefit greatly from a season of competition at higher levels.

The coaches also use the camp to work on technique, but then they are constantly stressing technique. A hand held inches too high, a turn not properly carved can cost mightily in a game where hundredths-of-a-second separate the winners from the also-rans.

After South America, there is a few week's rest, usually used to finish off schooling and to take part in a few dry land training camps. The season is fast approaching, so these camps can be tough. There's an element of fun skiing down even the toughest downhill course, but there's no fun in running up hills. This is where that constant conditioning in the spring pays off. And it pays off later, too, when you can walk away from a crashing tumble.

The time is also used by coaches and team officials to check on weather and snow conditions in Europe. They want to start on-snow training as soon as possible and get the team acclimatized to Europe. Often within three weeks of the South American camp, the World Cup squads will be heading for Europe.

The first few weeks in Europe are usually taken up with slalom and giant slalom training until there is enough snow on the longer downhill runs. The rigorous dry land training continues into November, then slackens off until you're doing only stretching and warmup exercises every day before putting on the skis. The season is about to begin. From now until March, you'll be racing or training almost every day, quite enough to maintain a high level of condition.

DOWNHILL RACING

The first time on a downhill course, speed isn't at all important. Looking around and learning the course is.

Racers have designated times for training on the course and, usually, will get only four to six runs on it before the race, depending on the snow conditions and the organizers' decision on how much punishment the course can take before it starts to break up.

Most racers have seen the course before, unless it's their first year on the circuit. The hills are the same year after year, and races are held at about the same time of the year on the same mountains.

Still, although there are usually few changes in the run, it is important to reconnoiter the course carefully the first time on it. Snow conditions can be vastly different from year to year and the slightest repositioning of a gate can drastically alter the line.

Training runs

The first run is to familiarize yourself with the course, the snow conditions and to think about the right line. The second time out, you start concentrating on speed as well as the correct line. More speed can make a difference to the line, making it necessary to start the turn earlier to scrub off enough speed to make it around.

Usually after two practice runs, the coach will tell you to "go for it this time," a common expression that needs no explanation. Now is the time to get down to business.

I believe a racer should put all he or she can into training runs to simulate, as closely as possible, the actual race. That way, when race day comes, there are no surprises. Loafing down a course is not the way to learn all its little secrets. Even a couple of miles an hour difference in speed can turn a tiny molehill into a mountain, or change a gentle turn into a horror.

Going all out also prepares you mentally for racing and builds confidence in your ability to handle the course. The confidence is important to be successful in any event. If you don't believe you can go fast enough to win, you won't. The confidence gained in a good, fast practice run also keeps the inevitable butterflies down on race day. A few butterflies are good to keep you alert, but extreme nervousness usually forebodes a disastrous race.

Knowing downhill courses was always a matter I took very seriously, and it probably paid large dividends in allowing me to get close to the top in downhill seedings. All through training, I would go over a downhill course in my mind time and time again. It was there in my head constantly.

Your times in practice are the best indicator of whether you are making mistakes, but the widespread use of videotape machines helps you to actually see where you're going wrong.

Coaches tape their own racers as well as the fastest racers from the other teams. This way, it's possible to actually pick out the fastest line through a turn.

And, of course, a racer can kid himself or herself about the mistakes, but it's tough to fool the videotape machine.

Downhill racing, especially, is a matter of eliminating the mistakes. Every skier makes them. Usually, the one who makes the fewest wins.

1 2

3 4

Starting procedure

In the race, getting a good start is vital. It is often won or lost right here. Racers come out of the starting gate at one-minute intervals. When one goes, the next steps into position. You get a signal at 30 seconds and another with 10 seconds to go. With five seconds to go, the starter begins a countdown: five-four-three-two-one-GO. Of course, the countdown can be in a foreign language, so it's a good idea to learn to count, at least to five, in a wide variety of languages.

On the GO, you lunge forward, pushing with all the strength in both your arms and legs. Your poles should start in front of you to give the strongest and longest possible thrust.

Then, you're skating, as hard and as far as you can to build up your speed as quickly as possible. As soon as you are going so fast that skating is no longer possible, you drop quickly into the downhill tuck. It's important to do this as quickly as possible. A split second delay in getting into the tuck is a split second lost, and races are often won or lost by hundredths, even thousandths, of a second.

1. Ready position. The feet should be right at the gate with the hands and poles ahead.

2. Just before the "go" signal, crouch back, ready to spring forward as hard as you can.

3. On the "go", thrust forward with the body. At the same time, pull with your arms and push with your legs. If you are doing it properly, the tails of your skis should kick up.

4. When you're through the starting gate, skate as hard as you can and push with your poles two or three times to quickly build up your momentum.

Downhill tuck

The modern tuck was developed in wind-tunnel tests and the idea is to break through the air as smoothly as possible. The tuck is the essence of modern downhill racing, every bit as important as good waxing, good skis, technique and courage combined.

Its importance is probably better illustrated by noting that the simple act of holding out a hand into the air stream at high speed can slow a racer as much as ten miles per hour!

Even the ski poles used by downhillers are bent so that they curve back behind the body, out of the air stream. The baskets are replaced by small balls to minimize the amount of air they catch. Downhill suits, too, are slick, form-fitting uniforms with no flaps or creases to catch the air.

On the straights, it's important that you ride on flat skis, that is, skis that are not edging.

If the edges are biting, it indicates you are slipping sideways and that's not the fastest way to get down the hill. It's especially important to ride a flat ski and avoid any mistakes when you are approaching a flat section. Going into a flat section, you should be carrying as much speed as possible. A mistake that slows you down has a multiplier effect on a slow stretch. It's not just the bit of speed you may lose going into the section, but the speed loss is increased all the way through it because you can never increase your speed through a flat section.

The same thing, in reverse, is true of speed you can gather coming out of a turn. The speed you gain increases proportionately through the next straight section.

Therefore, a racer should be back into a tuck as soon as possible after completing a turn. Going into the turn, the tuck should be held as long as possible and the ski allowed to run until the last possible instant before actually starting the turn.

In the perfect downhill tuck, you are presenting as small a frontal area as possible to the windstream. The hands should be held well out ahead to break the air. Your back should be flat and your head should be held up. The skis should run as flat as possible on the snow. Let your knees and ankles absorb the bumps.

The downhill line

The shortest distance between two points is a straight line, so it's vital that the turn or corner be straightened out as much as you can. Every corner, whether it be in downhill, slalom or giant slalom, has its line: an imaginary path that gets you through the corner quicker than any other route. In slalom or giant slalom, the line through one gate is often dictated by the path you must take to get to the next gate. But in downhill, usually corners are so far apart that they can be treated individually.

Almost always, coaches will set downhill gates so that you follow the natural path of the course down the hill. Therefore, the best line is usually the line you would take if there were no gates there at all.

Imagine you are about to take a right-hand turn in a downhill race. You would approach the turn as far to the outside (the left) as possible. The turn should take you from the outside of the course, across to a point at the apex of the turn on the inside (right side), then back out to the outside again, so that, in effect, you have turned the corner into a straight line as much as possible.

Naturally, snow conditions or bumps on the edge of the course will sometimes dictate a somewhat modified line.

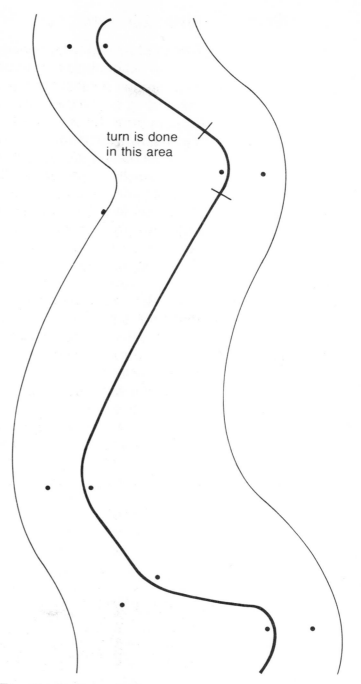

turn is done in this area

The illustration shows a typical section of a downhill course with the gates set up so that the path a skier must take follows the natural path of the hill. Turning high, or making the turn before you get to the gate, allows you to cover the least possible distance, an important consideration for a fast time.

THE SLALOM LINE

While the downhiller, in general, follows the natural course of the ski run, the slalom and giant slalom skier has a purely artificial route to take through a series of gates made up of poles stuck in the snow. Depending on the person who sets the course and the hill it's on, the run can be dead easy or extremely difficult. In either case, there are many slow ways through the course, but only one fast one: the Line.

Just as an auto racer follows a line through a corner, a ski racer must follow a predetermined line through a slalom course.

All top racers make a careful study of the course before a run to plan their line. Out of the starting gate, the experience racer "goes high" into the first gate, which simply means initiating the turn well before reaching the gate.

Inexperienced racers often head directly for the gate and don't start the turn until they reach it. It's too late then. It means the turn won't be completed until the racer is well past the gate and, therefore, the racer is poorly set up for the next one.

As you pass the inside pole of the gate, the turn should be almost complete and you should already be setting up for the next gate. In slalom racing, each turn should be made with the next gate in mind. For this reason, each turn is something of a compromise as you sacrifice the perfect line in order to be in line for the next gate. It's difficult at first, but top racers are looking ahead about three gates at all times to ensure they don't get caught off line.

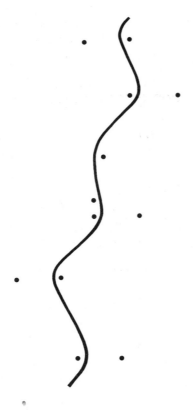

The slalom and giant slalom skier has a totally artificial line to follow through a series of gates. The gates are set up with no regard for the natural path down the hill and, more often than not, a racer must modify the fastest line through any gate in order to be in the best position to take the next gate. Each turn, therefore, is a compromise. Again, as in downhill racing, the turn is almost always completed before the skier actually reaches the gate. The difference is that the shape of the turn and the direction a skier is going when he or she passes the gate is determined by the location of the next gate.

Types of Gates

Slalom

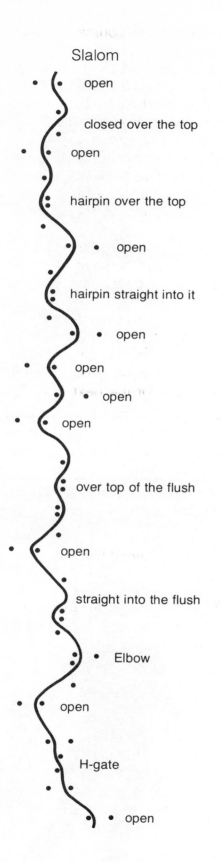

- open
- closed over the top
- open
- hairpin over the top
- open
- hairpin straight into it
- open
- open
- open
- open
- over top of the flush
- open
- straight into the flush
- Elbow
- open
- H-gate
- open

Downhill

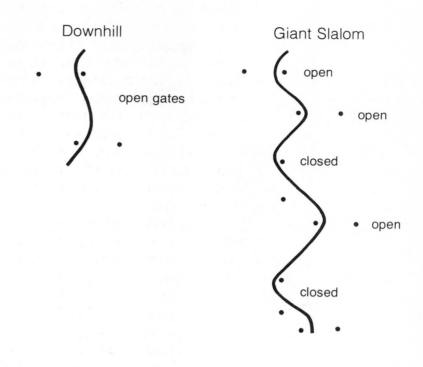

open gates

Giant Slalom

- open
- open
- closed
- open
- closed

Basically, there are only two types of gates, called "open" and "closed". All others are combinations of the basic pair. The open gate is one that is made up of poles that are lined across the hill, while the closed gate is made of poles running down the hill. Combinations of the two are used to create hairpins (two closed gates in a row), flushes (three closed in a row), Elbows (open and closed combined) and H-gates (an open, a closed and another open all in a row). Only open gates are used in downhill racing. All types, except flushes, are used in giant slalom. All of them are used to confound the slalom racer. Gates are also set up so that a skier must enter from different positions. For instance, if it is necessary to cross over the top of a gate to get through it, it would be described as an "over the top" gate. Often, this means an extra turn to get through it. When the gate is set up to allow you to get through it following the natural course you are on, it's called going "straight into" a gate.

1 2

3 4

GIANT SLALOM

Sometimes a giant slalom course is set the day before a race, but usually you won't get to see it until the morning of the race. Rules prevent you from skiing through the gates, but you are allowed to sideslip down the course to inspect it.

Look the course over as much as time permits before you have to ski it. Memorize the gate sequences, so you know where to go with absolutely no hesitation. This also includes memorizing the line, planning exactly where you're going to turn and exactly the point where you should be initiating the turn.

Take note of the bumps and ripples in the course, keeping in mind that the next time you see them you'll be going at high speed and if they come as a surprise to you, you're going to get into trouble.

Women's giant slaloms are usually only a single run, while men have two runs. The number of runs doesn't matter, really, as far as mistakes are concerned. Almost any serious error will cost you any chance of winning or placing high.

The GS is run at speeds of about 30 to 45 mph, pretty fast when you're on skis and are expected to make instant decisions on turns.

On the World Cup circuit, the coach will usually set up a short training course so the team can go through the same sort of gates they will run in the race. It helps to loosen up the racer before the competition and also sets the mood — aggressiveness.

The aggressiveness is important. You have to charge and forget all about falling.

You concentrate on turning high and early for the gates, unless the course calls for a delayed turn and you concentrate on staying on the downhill ski.

This is no time to worry about technique or errors. This should come automatically at this stage.

You may remember your errors and technical mistakes after, but during a race they would be too much to think about.

1. In a slalom or giant slalom, you must race as close to the poles as possible to make a straight line out of the course. The arms are well out ahead, literally pointing the way and not somewhere at your side where they can catch on a pole. Also, holding them well out in front almost guarantees you will remain well forward on your skis.

2. As you come past the gate, all your weight is on the lower ski. Then, you should begin to switch the weight to the other ski and drive with the knee.

3. Look ahead at all times. When the turn is fully completed—and only then — you should skate into the next gate.

4. If you begin to skate, though, before the turn is completed, your ski will slide and you will lose time.

SLALOM

Almost all slaloms are two runs with your total time counting, which means you must turn in two near-perfect runs to stand a chance of winning.

Again, you are not allowed to ski through the gates on either of the courses before the race, nor are you allowed to "shadow" the course, which is skiing down alongside it, simulating the actual run.

Some skiers will sideslip down a slalom run, but most memorize the course by climbing up through the gates. This helps you to memorize the gates and the combinations. Every gate on the course and its relationship to the other gates must be firmly planted in your mind, ready to be played back like a videotape when you're racing. In slalom, because the gates are so close together, they come up very fast. Sometimes it feels like you're trying to ski through the posts on a picket fence.

Climbing up the hill, you should note delayed turns, spots where ice may increase your speed and, of course, on which side of a gate to go. Coaches also set up courses resembling the real thing for practice which help you get your rhythm.

In a high-speed turn, it's not necessary to come as close to the pole as in a slalom. It's more important that most of the turn is completed before you reach the pole; therefore, it is necessary to set up early. Again, as you pass the pole, your weight should be almost entirely on the outside ski, and your hands should be well out in front. When the turn is fully completed, a slight step in the direction of the next turn will get you set up for it as soon as possible.

The key to quick slalom is to concentrate on quick knee movements and keep the hands well out ahead to keep you forward on the skis.

If you successfully complete the first run, which means you haven't missed a gate or failed to complete the course, you should climb up again and memorize the second course. This can only be done between runs. It's too much to attempt to memorize two courses and it lessens the chance of confusing the two.

In slalom racing, there's no chance to "cool it." It's an all-out charge because the competition in the upper levels of ski racing is fierce. Even if you've won the first round, the calibre of the competition is so high that you can't afford to slack off on the second.

Prejumping

At high speed, a bump can easily throw a skier out of control or throw you high into the air and cost you speed. Prejumping helps to maintain control and speed.

It's a method whereby you jump over the upward slope of a bump, or mogul, and land on the downward side. The force of landing on the downward side should increase your speed and you avoid the shock of hitting the upward slope at high speed. Naturally, timing is all important. A misjudged prejump can be disastrous.

FINISHING

The finish of any race is almost as important as the start. When you're through the final gate of a slalom or giant slalom you should be skating hard for the line, pushing with every stride and driving with your pole. Easing off at the finish can cost valuable fractions, so you should never give up until you are well past the finish line.

Often, you will see determined racers jump into the air just before they reach the finish line in an attempt to break the timing beam with the fronts of their skis. Ski racing is so close that often this can be the difference between a gold medal and a second place.

Sometimes, in a downhill race, a strong finish will mean holding a tuck until you are well through the electric eyes at the finish.

Chapter 6
CROSS-
COUNTRY
SKIING

EQUIPMENT

As a family pastime, part of the great appeal of cross-country skiing is that equipment and clothing are considerably less expensive than that for alpine skiing. Other obvious savings include lighter travel costs and no need to buy lift tickets.

Cross-country clothing

Because you generate your own heat through body movement, cross-country garb should be lightweight and loose-fitting.

Materials that absorb perspiration are essential, so avoid waterproof garments that don't breathe and thus keep perspiration in.

Although clothing designers have started to pay much closer attention to cross-country skiing and are now producing stylish touring outfits, just about anything goes on the trails.

Personally, I prefer a sweatsuit. It's not glamorous, but it's loose and absorbs the perspiration.

Knickers, of course, are traditional and, with long socks, are ideal. Don't, whatever you do, wear ski pants. They don't breathe very well and the elastic material has to stretch with every step. They will tire you very quickly.

I'd suggest two pair of socks — first, they breathe better, and secondly, they help prevent blisters. If it's really cold, an old pair of woolen socks with the toes cut out can be pulled over the boots for extra warmth.

A lightweight wool hat that can be tugged over the ears and light wool mitts are the other essentials.

When I go cross-country skiing, I carry a small pack which contains a light jacket or shell, handy items to prevent chills when I stop for lunch or a break, and also a spare sweater and an apple or sandwich for snacking.

Cross-country skis

Cross-country skis are divided into two main categories, general-touring and light-touring. It's important to get the right kind for the type of skiing you'll be doing.

On the left is the light-touring type of ski, noticeably narrower than the general-touring ski on the right. The light-touring is by far the more popular because of its versatility and because it is less tiring.

Light-touring skis are the narrower of the two types. They are not as stable as general-touring skis, which are noticeably heavier and wider. On the other hand, the light-touring models don't tire you as easily on long trips and day tours.

Most people start out with lighter skis because of their versatility. They even can be used for racing, although special racing skis are lighter and narrower still.

The traditional hickory skis are quickly giving way to fiberglass, which is lighter than wood and, because of its surface qualities, eliminates much of the need for waxing.

The type of ski is a matter of personal preference. Length, though, is dictated by the skier's proficiency.

A novice should have skis 4 inches above the head; an intermediate's should be 8 inches taller; and experts pick skis from 10 to 15 inches taller than they are.

Camber, or the flex of the ski, is important. Here's a simple test: put on the skis indoors and place a sheet of paper under the center of the ski, right below your foot. You should be able to pull one sheet out from under the ski. Three or four sheets will be too tight to pull out.

Boots and poles

Like skis, cross-country boots fall into light-touring and general-touring categories. It's important that the boots you pick match the type of ski you've selected.

The general-touring boot is heavier, has higher sides and is stronger and stiffer than a light-touring boot. It is used with a heel cable, or what is called a Kandahar binding.

The lighter boot is lower, ending just below the ankle. It's more flexible and uses a toe-clamp binding.

The lighter boot with the simple toe binding is by far the most popular.

To get a good fit, remember to take two pairs of socks with you when trying on the boots. Most people wear two pairs to keep warm and to prevent blisters.

In selecting poles, there are three important considerations: get them strong, light and the right length.

Aluminum poles are the best buy. They're lighter than bamboo and don't break as easily.

Poles should be long enough so that they reach from the floor to fit snugly in the underarm.

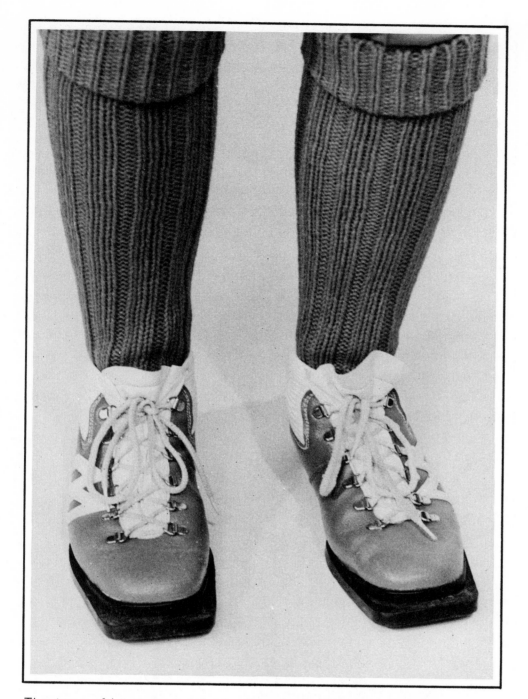

The type of boot you pick should match the type of ski. This is a light-touring boot. It is very flexible and has an extended sole which fits into a toe-clamp binding.

Aluminum poles, shown here on the left, are a better choice than bamboo, on the right, because they are lighter and stronger.

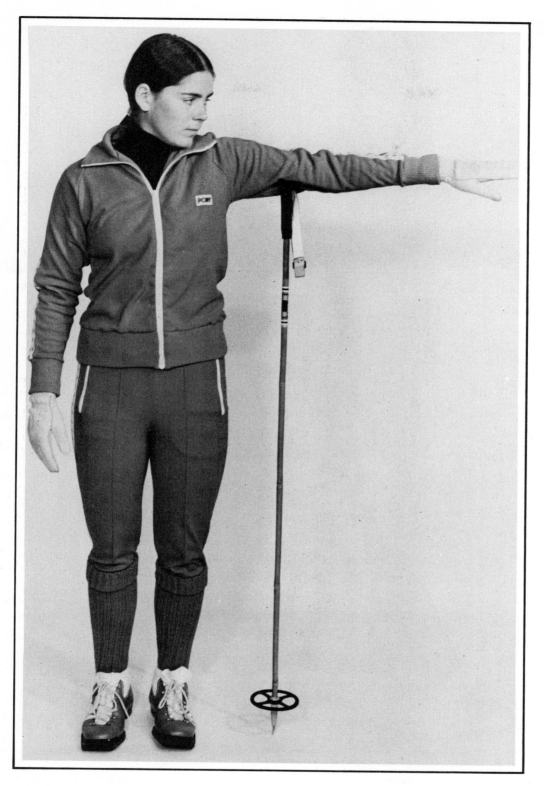

This is the proper method to determine the length of your poles. They should reach from the floor to fit snugly under your arm.

THE BASIC STRIDE

Done well, cross-country skiing looks as easy as walking. In fact, it is, as long as you have a bit of guidance to get you started.

The basic stride in cross-country skiing is just a slight adaptation of the basic stride in walking.

Begin on a flat surface by simply walking around and sliding on your skis. If you have done some alpine skiing, the sensation of having long boards on your feet will not be new. Otherwise, it takes a bit of getting used to.

You also have to get accustomed to your heel lifting off the ski when you step.

Beginners make the common error of trying to lift the ski off the snow. The forward stride, though, is not a lift, but a push. The skis should always remain on the snow with the feet in a normal walking position about 12 inches apart.

It is easier to ski in a track. At the beginning, follow in someone else's track or put on your skis and press down the snow to make a short track of your own. If you make your own track, you've already started to ski.

The basic stride is a normal walking stride, your left leg and right arm going forward together and vice versa.

However, instead of lifting your rear foot completely, as you would in walking, you lift only the heel, then push forward.

The movement is a definite stride, not a shuffle. You don't shuffle when you walk, so don't do it when you ski.

The basic stride in cross-country skiing is just a slight adaptation of the basic walking stride. However, instead of lifting your rear foot completely as you would in walking, you lift only the heel and push forward. Remember, it's a definite stride, not a shuffle.

STEPPING A TURN

The basic turn in cross-country skiing is called the step turn or, when at a complete standstill, the star turn (so named because of the pattern you leave in the snow).

In either case, it's a series of steps, the number depending on how far you want to turn.

To make a left turn, for instance, you step the left ski in the direction of the turn. Not too far, though, because that throws you off balance and creates a tendency to cross skis. A good rule is to keep the tails of your skis in contact with the snow at all times so you don't cross them.

The next step brings the right ski parallel with the left. When this is done, in effect you have just completed a small turn.

Repeat the two steps—left ski first, then bring the right ski over to join it—until you have turned as far as you want to go.

The step turn (or star turn) is a series of steps, the number depending on how far you want to turn. Step the ski in the direction you wish to turn, then bring the other ski up until it's parallel with the first. In effect, you have just completed a small turn. Don't step too far at any one time because this tends to throw you off balance. A series of these steps allows you to turn as far as you desire.

STOPPING

Because it works so well in the confined space of cross-country trails, the snowplow is by far the best method of stopping.

The idea is to get the skis into a "V" and use them the way you would use the blades of a plow, to dig into the snow.

The force needed to get the skis into the snowplow position comes from the knees and the heels, the knees pushing down and in and the heels pushing out.

The tips of the skis should remain fairly close together while the tails fan out to form the "V".

The more pressure you apply at the knees, the quicker the stop.

Any turn can be applied to stop you, providing the hill is wide enough. To use a turn to stop, you simply carry the turn through until you are pointed back up the hill.

The snowplow can slow you or stop you in the confined space of cross-country trails. Get the skis into a "V" by pushing forward and in with the knees. The tips should be close together with the tails of the skis fanned out behind. The more pressure you apply with your knees, the quicker you will stop.

GLIDING

Sliding—or as it's called in cross-country skiing, gliding—moves you faster and with a lot less effort than just stepping over the snow.

It's important for beginners to learn to glide without the use of poles. This forces you to use your legs, which is where the glide should come from rather than from the push of the poles.

Pole thrust can be added later to lengthen the glide.

Start with your knees slightly bent. Step forward with one ski, keeping it on the snow. You will be able to feel the glide, or after-motion, which is a natural result of the forward thrust.

Wait until you have stopped gliding, then repeat with the other ski.

Now, the idea is to put them together without a stop between strides. Stride-glide-stride-glide. A bit faster each time until it becomes a natural movement.

At first, try not to over-emphasize the glide. It should be a quick, rhythmic motion.

As the glide becomes more natural, you will find that greater forward lean of the body and a pronounced arm swing will add thrust to your forward movement. To determine the correct amount of forward lean, let the upper body follow a straight line with the rear leg when you are in full stride.

Gliding is the simple process of letting your natural forward motion move you over the snow easier and quicker than you could with deliberate, stop-start steps. When you step forward, you will feel the natural tendency for your skis to slide ahead. When you have stopped gliding, repeat with the other ski. Now, put them together without a pronounced stop between them. Stride-glide-stride-glide. As it becomes more natural, a greater forward lean of the body and a more pronounced arm swing will add thrust to your forward movement.

SKATING TURN

Skaters should have no trouble learning this turn on cross-country skis, because it's almost exactly what they would do to make a turn on skates.

Called the skating turn, it's the basic step turn adapted to the glide through the unweighting and weighting of the skis.

As you push off on one ski, the other is completely unweighted and stepped in the direction you want to go.

The weight is then transferred to the ski that has made the turn. The other ski is brought parallel, and you are skiing in the new direction. To turn even more, you simply repeat the process.

The turn can be accomplished while skiing down a hill in the normal running position. Shift your total weight onto one ski, then push off on the weighted ski. Turn the unweighted ski in the new direction and shift the weight to it. You will then be able to bring the other ski parallel and head in the new direction.

The skating turn is really an adaptation of the step turn, the difference being that it's adapted to the glide through the weighting and unweighting of the skis. As you push off on one ski, as you would in the normal gliding motion, the other ski is completely unweighted and stepped in the direction you want to go. The weight is then transferred to the ski that has made the turn and the other is brought parallel, allowing you to ski off in the new direction.

CLIMBING

Cross-country implies skiing on flats, skiing downhill and climbing uphill. The latter is by far the most challenging.

Yet, facing even steep hills need not be a traumatic experience if you remember that climbing on skis employs the same principles as climbing on foot. And, besides, you have your poles to help.

Gradual inclines can be conquered with the basic cross-country stride, eliminating the gliding, of course.

Strides should be shorter, just as they normally are when you're walking up a hill. Poles should not be planted as far forward as in striding on the flat. In fact, the pole should not go in front of the forward foot. At least one pole is always firmly planted in the snow.

Knees should be bent more, and you should employ considerably more forward lean.

For steeper hills, the herringbone is employed. It's a reverse of the snow plow with the "V" formed behind you. In the herringbone climb, the poles are always planted behind the skis to prevent sliding back down the hill.

Finally, the steepest hills will require the side-step method, which is approximately the same movements you would make to climb sideways up a flight of stairs. At least one pole is always firmly planted in the snow, for obvious reasons.

WAXING

Ski waxing is an artform and, carried to the ultimate, requires a great deal of technique and experience.

Fortunately, the beginner need not fret too much about the finer points, because there are now kits on the market that take most of the worry out of waxing. Also, most waxes are color-coded, which is a help to the novice.

The beginner can get by with two types of waxes, one for wet snow (above freezing) and the other for dry snow (below 32 degrees F.).

To check snow, squeeze a handful in your gloves. If it packs, it's wet; it it blows away, it's dry.

For wet snow, a skier should apply soft wax, also called klister-wax. It is usually coded red, green or yellow.

Hard waxes, usually blue, are for use in dry snow.

A third type, for snow right around the 32-degree F. mark, is coded in purple.

The colors vary, though, but most waxing kits will spell out the temperatures right on the wax sticks or tubes.

A couple of words of caution about waxing:

1. Don't try to apply wax on dirty skis, especially those that have been carried on roof racks and exposed to road dirt.
2. Wax inside. It's more comfortable, and heated wax applies easier.
3. Soft wax can be applied right over hard wax, but the reverse is not true. Soft wax must be removed before a hard wax application.

If you follow a few simple waxing rules, it can add greatly to your enjoyment of cross-country skiing. With kits that are now on the market, even the novice can become an expert waxer with little trouble.

796.93   Crawford, Judy
Cr   SKIING BASICS